THE ZULU KINGDOM

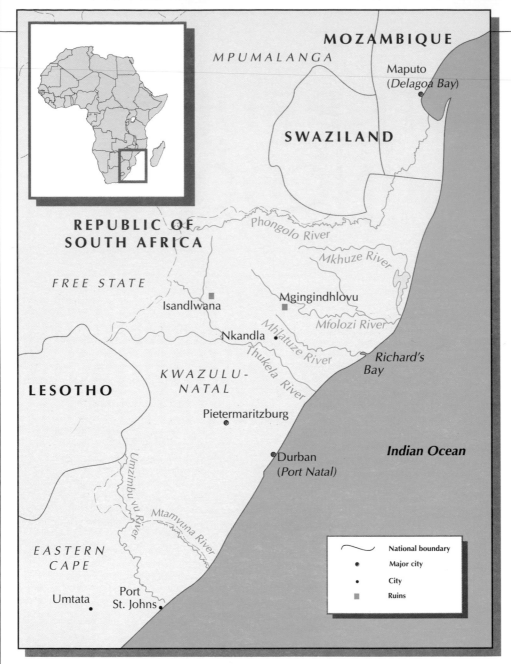

The area controlled by the Zulu Kingdom lay roughly between the Mkhuze River in the north and the Thukela River in the south.

~African Civilizations~

THE ZULU KINGDOM

Sandra Klopper, Ph.D.

A First Book

Franklin Watts
A Division of Grolier Publishing
New York / London / Hong Kong / Sydney
Danbury, Connecticut

Library of Congress Cataloging-in-Publication Data

Klopper, Sandra.
    The Zulu kingdom / Sandra Klopper. — 1st ed.
      p.   cm. — (African civilizations) (A first book)
    Includes bibliographical references and index.
    Summary: A survey of the history and culture of the Zulu kingdom
that emerged between 1816 and 1818 on the east coast of southern
Africa under the leadership of King Shaka.
    ISBN 0-531-20286-0
    1. Zulu (African people)—History—Juvenile literature. [1. Zulu
(African people)—History.]   I. Title. II. Series. III. Series: A first
book.
DT1768.Z95K47   1998
968.4'04—dc21

                              97-34574
                                 CIP
                                 AC

CONTENTS

INTRODUCTION

The Zulu Kingdom emerged between 1816 and 1818 on the east coast of southern Africa under the leadership of King Shaka (pronounced sha-GAH). Shaka was the son of Sezangakhona Zulu, who ruled the small Zulu *chiefdom*.

Shaka was a military genius and a powerful statesman. Overpowering his smaller neighbors, he absorbed them into the Zulu chiefdom. In this way he put together a large army that became famous—and feared—throughout southern Africa in the 1820s. The Zulu chiefdom became a powerful kingdom. Many weaker chiefs and their followers went into hiding or fled the region.

Shaka was assassinated in 1828 by warriors acting on behalf of his half-brother, Dingane (ding-GUN-he). After Shaka's death, Dingane ruled for twelve

Tradition and economic opportunity blend in modern South Africa. This Zulu man earns money entertaining tourists. Shaka and his successors formerly ruled the area in which beadwork designs of this type were later created.

A British magistrate collects taxes from the Zulu in 1879, the year that the Anglo-Zulu war broke out. British taxation was one of many causes that led to war. Each Zulu man is wearing an *isicoco*, a coiled head-ring.

years. Then he, too, was overthrown by another half-brother named Mpande (mm-PAN-deh) in 1840. Mpande controlled the kingdom for thirty-three years. He was succeeded by his son, Cetshwayo (SECH-why-oh), the last king to rule the Zulu Kingdom.

The Zulu Kingdom was defeated and destroyed by the British in the Anglo-Zulu war of 1879. After that, the British controlled the territory, although they allowed Cetshwayo to return as king. Since that

King Goodwill Zwelethini is the current Zulu king.

time Zulu kings have been ceremonial leaders without political power, much like European kings and queens. Shaka's twentieth-century descendants—King Solomon, King Cyprian, and King Goodwill Zwelethini—have all continued to guide their people in spiritual matters and to take part in important ceremonies.

Today, the region once ruled by Shaka is part of the Republic of South Africa. There, Shaka's achievements are annually honored on Heritage Day, September 24. It is the anniversary of Shaka's assassination.

1 TRADITIONS AND DAILY LIFE

In the Zulu language, *izulu* means "sky." The Zulu people, or amaZulu, once believed that their ancestors lived in the sky. According to their *creation myth*, iNkosi (God) became annoyed at a young man who repeatedly stole iNkosi's favorite ox and rode around on it. This young man was sent down to earth so that he would not cause trouble in the sky anymore. A hole was opened in the floor of the sky, and the young man was lowered through it onto the earth. Later, God sent a young woman to live with this man so that they could have many children. This is how the Zulu nation came into being.

To this day, some Zulu-speaking people believe that the stars are small holes in the floor of the sky

Traditionally, Zulu boys looked after their family's herd animals. Today most Zulu children attend school and wear Western clothes.

made by the hooves of God's cattle, and that the earth itself is held up by four bulls that carry it on their horns. When one of these bulls shakes its head, the earth also shakes. This is believed to be the cause of earthquakes.

As these myths suggest, cattle were central to the lives of the Zulu. A man with many cattle always had the respect of his neighbors. During the day, young boys took the cows and goats out to graze and to drink water from the nearby rivers. Although these animals were milked every day, they were slaughtered and eaten only on ritual occasions in memory of the ancestors. The Zulu therefore ate very little meat, which was considered a luxury food. Their daily diet generally consisted of *amasi,* or sour milk; a porridge made from corn; a root vegetable known as *idumbe*; and, less often, beans, pumpkins, edible greens, and *amakhowe*, large, tasty mushrooms that grew wild.

MARRIAGE TRADITIONS

Young men often still follow a custom called *ilobolo*. This requires a groom to give a number of cattle to the father of his bride. In exchange, the bride usually brings presents for her future parents-in-law, including blankets and cooking pots. In the past she also brought headrests, or wooden head supports used when sleeping, for her husband and herself.

Hairstyles were a key sign of age and marital status in the Zulu Kingdom. When men married they began wearing a coiled head-ring, or *isicoco*. This coil was rolled from a gum-like substance obtained from

Hairstyles were important indicators both of a woman's marital status and of the region from which she came. These married Zulu women come from different areas.

a plant, then sewn onto the man's hair to prevent the *isicoco* from falling off.

A married woman also changed her hairstyle. Shortly before her wedding, she let her hair grow; then she tied it into a knot on top of her head. This knot was usually powdered with red ocher, a type of colored earth.

In the nineteenth century a newly married Zulu couple first went to live in the *homestead* of the bridegroom's family.

HOMESTEADS

Usually, six or more thatched, beehive-shaped houses were in each homestead. A large, circular corral was placed at the center of this group of houses, where goats and cows were shielded from attack by lions and leopards at night. Homesteads were situated some distance apart from one another. They were surrounded by large grassland areas reserved for grazing the goats and cows.

The homesteads of the Zulu kings were also arranged around a circular enclosure. Unlike homesteads of the common people they consisted of two separate sections: a large royal enclosure, or *isigodlo*, occupied by the king and other members of the royal family, and a massive military barracks. The barracks were occupied by young Zulu men, all of whom were *conscripted* into the army when they were still in their teens.

Zulu houses were designed to stay cool in summer and warm in winter. They were exceptionally effective. The remarkable success of their design owes to the fact that they were completely covered in *thatching grass*, which is an excellent form of *insulation*. The small semicircular doorway at one end and the

A traditional Zulu house. Cattle horns are placed above the entrance of Zulu homesteads.

absence of windows also helped to regulate the temperature. Fires for cooking were lit in the center of the house. The smoke escaped through the thatch.

THE RISE OF THE ZULU KINGDOM

Sezangakhona Zulu was the father of Shaka, Dingane, and Mpande and the head of a small chiefdom close to the Mfolozi River. He had many wives, including Shaka's mother, Nandi, Dingane's mother, Mpikase, and Mpande's mother, Songiya. In those days, marrying the daughters of neighboring chiefs was an important practice because it helped to build good relations between different chiefdoms.

In the region surrounding the Zulu chiefdom were many other chiefdoms whose peoples all shared a broadly similar culture and spoke closely related languages. Together these peoples are sometimes called the North Nguni (nn-GOO-nee). Like the Zulu,

A rare drawing of King Shaka made by a British trader who had met him

these small groups had probably migrated to southern Africa from central Africa more than a thousand years earlier.

SHAKA AS CHIEF

When Shaka became chief of the Zulu, he attacked these neighboring groups and forced them to join him. He wanted the Zulu Kingdom to become powerful enough to control trade in the region.

At this time, the early nineteenth century, the key trade routes in the region led north to Delagoa Bay (present-day Maputo, Mozambique). Delagoa Bay was run by the Portuguese and was the site of trade between Africa and Europe. The Portuguese traded European beads, woven cloth, and various metals. In exchange they received African cattle, elephant ivory, and animal skins.

The Zulu themselves did not have the technology to make glass beads, and they did not grow the cotton needed to weave cotton cloth, so cloth and glass beads were particularly valuable to them. The Zulu also found it convenient to trade their cattle for metals instead of producing metal themselves. This meant that Zulu blacksmiths could concentrate on making things—such as spears, hoes, and brass ornaments—rather than on locating ore.

During Shaka's rule, the European goods obtained from Delagoa Bay were brought to the

Baskets played religious and everyday roles in Zulu culture.

king's royal homestead by some of the men attached to his army.

After trading at Delagoa Bay, these soldiers also collected goods from the Tsonga people, who lived in the area between the Zulu Kingdom and the Portuguese settlement. To avoid being attacked by Shaka's army, the Tsonga were forced to supply the Zulu royal family with such handmade goods as baskets, decorated *gourds*, and carved sticks.

The Zulu royal family had many uses for the Tsonga baskets. Some served as grain containers. Others were beer baskets, woven tightly enough to hold a fermented, beer-like drink brewed from millet. Millet beer was drunk during religious ceremonies in praise of the dead. Deceased ancestors were believed to assist and protect their living descendants. The king's ancestors were the most important of all. It was believed that Shaka's control over the Zulu Kingdom came as much from the powerful spiritual help of his ancestors as from his warriors.

The sticks that Tsonga sculptors carved for Shaka and the Zulu royal family were status symbols. They were decorated with complex, abstract shapes.

SHAKA'S ARMY

Many Tsonga sticks ended up in the Zulu Kingdom. Most were not status symbols for the royal family, however, but heavy clubs with bulbous heads, called knobkerries. Every member of Shaka's large army had knobkerries for hunting and for fighting enemies in close combat. Zulu soldiers also carried shields and spears.

The thousands of soldiers who lived in Shaka's barracks were often sent out to raid cattle from people to the east and south of the Zulu Kingdom. The rest of their time was spent training for combat,

In addition to their combat uniforms, Zulu warriors often wore special uniforms for Zulu ceremonies. Shaka's nephew wearing his ceremonial uniform, which included a shield, beads, feathers, and animal skin.

The framework of traditional Zulu houses consists of long, straight saplings that are bent into a beehive shape.

looking after the king's cornfields, or helping to build new military settlements in other parts of the Zulu Kingdom. Huge amounts of building material had to be collected for this purpose. Regiments, therefore, spent a lot of their time walking to and from the Nkandla Forest to look for the long, straight saplings needed to make frames for their thatched houses.

Warriors were formed into large regiments and were allowed to marry only when the king gave them permission. This meant that most warriors were over the age of thirty before they left the king's royal homestead to build their own homesteads.

King Shaka was much stricter in applying these rules than any of his successors. Partly for this reason, he is remembered as a very hard man who seldom showed pity or concern for others.

Yet in some ways he was very vulnerable. He was terrified of growing old, and he was fiercely protective of his mother, Nandi. When Nandi died, he forced the entire kingdom to join him in mourning her death.

3 DINGANE

When Dingane became king in 1828, he moved his royal homestead to the northeast of where Shaka's capital had been. He called his homestead Mgingindhlovu (mm-gin-gind-LAW-vu), meaning "the place of the elephants."

TRADE

For the next twelve years Mgingindhlovu was a hive of activity. Here, Dingane entertained visitors from as far afield as present-day Botswana, hundreds of miles to the northeast. He also conducted a thriving trade with British merchants who had settled to the south of the kingdom in 1824. Their settlement at

King Dingane often wore this blue cloak, which was given to him by a European visitor.

Port Natal (present-day Durban, South Africa) was much nearer to the Zulu Kingdom than was Delagoa Bay. For this reason, British traders quickly replaced the Portuguese as the main European trading partners of Shaka and his successors.

DINGANE'S REGIMENTS

No one knows how or why Dingane persuaded three important leaders in the Zulu army to kill Shaka. Dingane probably wanted to restore peace after the destructive wars his half-brother had fought in the early 1820s. Peace proved difficult to achieve, however, for many of Dingane's generals were not prepared to follow Dingane's instructions. Even so, Dingane was very popular with his regiments. He made sure that they always had more than enough food, including meat, and he relaxed some of the harsh restrictions Shaka had placed on young men in the Zulu army.

Dingane's regiments each had a different uniform with an elaborate headdress made from otter or leopard skins and various kinds of feathers, including ostrich feathers. These uniforms were not worn in combat but on important ceremonial occasions.

CHIEFDOMS NEAR THE KINGDOM

Like Shaka, Dingane still sent his regiments on military expeditions, but he was generally quite tolerant of neighboring peoples. For example, he encouraged various communities that had gone into hiding during Shaka's rule to rebuild their homesteads and replant their cornfields. Most of these groups lived to the south of the Thukela River, beyond the borders of the Zulu Kingdom.

But in return for Dingane's protection, they were required to supply him with *tribute*—payments of cattle and such other valuable goods as animal pelts and the colorful feathers that were worn on ceremonial occasions by the king and his warriors. In this way these communities on the edges of Zulu territory fell under Zulu control, although the control there was less strict than in the heart of the Zulu Kingdom. These communities spent so much of their time hunting for feathers and furs for the Zulu Kingdom that they had little time left to tend their fields and look after their own needs. As a result, they sometimes lacked adequate food and clothing.

Those Zulu-speaking communities to the south of the kingdom shared several customs with their neighbors in the Zulu Kingdom. Like the Zulu, they did not practice male circumcision, which was common among other southern African groups, including the Tsonga. In addition, they organized their regiments into age grades: Men of more or less the same age were brought together in regiments.

However, the chiefs who ruled south of the Thukela River had much less power over their communities than did the Zulu kings. For example, these chiefs were unable to make young men follow the rule that they had to keep their heads shaved until they married. Defiant young men adopted *nonconformist* hairstyles. These hairstyles resembled the punk hairstyles that became popular among young British men and women in the 1980s. Both groups used their hairstyles as a way of marking their differences from their parents' generation.

THE FIRST FRUITS CEREMONY

The most important annual event in the Zulu Kingdom was the First Fruits Ceremony, which was held immediately after the first large harvest of the summer season. This event was designed to highlight the king's key role in all religious matters. The regi-

Many young men in Zulu-influenced chiefdoms south of the Thukela River defied their rulers by wearing nonconformist hairstyles such as this.

Zulu soldiers were sometimes required to sing and dance for the king as a sign of loyalty. Their dancing shields (above) were much smaller than their fighting shields.

ments were required to perform songs and dances as a sign of their continuing loyalty to the king.

Preparations for the First Fruits Ceremony began about a month before the harvest. During Dingane's reign, every regiment from across the Zulu Kingdom gathered at Mgingindhlovu, where they spent time working in the king's fields, readying their ceremonial uniforms, and practicing new songs and dances.

Early on the morning of the appointed day, the

king emerged from the royal enclosure. He was dressed in a costume made from the fibers of various plants, and his face was painted red, white, and black. Holding a sacred spear with a crescent-shaped blade in his right hand, he spat a mixture of medicinal herbs at the rising sun. It was believed that this action ensured the support of the powerful royal ancestors for a successful harvest the following year.

The king used the First Fruits Ceremony to distribute gifts of furs and feathers and, in some cases, brass neck-rings and armbands to his regiments. In return the regiments brought pieces of straw from their thatched huts and scrapings from the wooden posts of their homestead doorways. These were included in a large coiled ring known as the *inkatha* (in-KAHT-ah), which symbolized the unity and strength of the Zulu nation. The *inkatha* was housed in a sacred shelter in the king's royal enclosure, or *isigodlo*. Whenever the Zulu were at war, the king sat on the *inkatha* to help ensure his army's victory.

THE BOERS

In the 1830s, *Boers*—white settlers of mostly Dutch background—lived more than 1,000 miles (1,600 km) southwest of the Zulu Kingdom. They had settled in the British colony at the Cape of Good Hope. But the Boers decided to leave the colony because they were not prepared to accept Britain's decision to free all slaves. They completely disagreed with the idea that blacks and whites could ever be equal. To escape British control, which they deeply resented, the Boers trekked northeast, traveling in ox wagons across the interior of southern Africa.

A large group of the migrating Boers reached the Zulu Kingdom and decided it was a perfect place to settle. They pressured Dingane to grant them rights of residence on the edge of the kingdom. At first Dingane reluctantly agreed. Later, however, he reversed his decision. In 1838, when a Boer negotiating party visited his royal homestead, he ordered his soldiers to execute them.

Historians are still debating Dingane's motives. Some think he was threatened by the Boers' military power. Their guns and horses enabled them to defeat African armies that fought on foot with spears.

After the death of their party at Mgingindhlovu, the Boers declared war on Dingane. They enlisted the help of his half-brother, Mpande, by promising to make him king. Over the next two years, the Zulu and the Boers fought several battles.

When the armed Boer commando, or war party, finally reached Mgingindhlovu to avenge the death of their friends and bury them, Dingane and his followers prepared to flee the royal homestead. They packed their personal belongings as quickly as they could, tying them up in bundles or putting them in baskets. They gathered their headrests, eating utensils, sleeping mats, the costumes worn at the First Fruits Ceremony, and as much food as they could carry. They opened the royal corral and drove Dingane's cattle to safety before burning down Dingane's personal dwelling.

The Zulu believed that anything belonging to the king contained powerful substances that could be used to make medicines or magic potions that might kill him and his people. This explains why Dingane's personal dwelling was burned.

Dingane fled from his burning capital. He died in exile in 1840, probably at the hands of his enemies

One clash between the Zulu and the Boers, known as the Battle of Blood River, is famous. There the Boers defeated the Zulu. The descendants of the

Boers killed in that battle viewed it as having almost religious significance, "proof" of their belief that whites were superior to blacks. In the twentieth century the battle was honored by the *apartheid* government of South Africa as a public holiday. We now know that the Battle of Blood River was just one of several battles that led to Dingane's defeat.

DINGANE'S LEGACY

Dingane is now most often remembered for the murder of the Boers at Mgingindhlovu, but he also deserves to be remembered for his positive achievements. Apart from the First Fruits Ceremony—the only event that brought the entire kingdom together every year—Dingane also organized large cultural events at Mgingindhlovu on other occasions. He was a great patron of the arts and took a personal interest in all forms of culture. He encouraged the development of singing and dramatic dancing displays, in which he himself participated. He also took great pleasure in wearing beautifully sewn necklaces and armbands made from imported glass beads.

Dingane was the first Zulu king who was forced to deal with the threat of white settlers armed with

King Dingane, dressed for a dance at the capital. His clothing features fur, feathers, and bead-work; his armbands are made of ivory and metal. Dingane is said to have liked these drawings, although they were not accurate likenesses of him, because they realistically depicted his attire.

weapons that were much more effective than the spears and knobkerries of the Zulu regiments. Though his confrontation with the white settlers led to Dingane's defeat, future Zulu kings fared little better against settlers, whether they used military force or diplomacy.

4 MISSIONARIES AND SETTLERS

The Boers who visited Dingane in 1838 were not the only white people who posed a threat to the Zulu Kingdom. The Zulu also grew more and more suspicious of the British who had settled at Port Natal.

When British traders first visited the Zulu Kingdom in 1824 they were welcomed with open arms. But over time it became clear that they were not prepared to obey the king's instruction that they trade only with him. Instead of going directly to the king's royal homestead, they began to trade with the heads of families living in homesteads scattered throughout the kingdom. As a result, the

Zulu people no longer depended on the king for such luxury items as beads and such vital tools as metal hoes. This damaged the prestige and control of the king, who slowly lost his power over his people.

MISSIONARIES

During the reign of the third Zulu king, Mpande, another problem emerged. White missionaries tried to set up Christian mission stations in the Zulu Kingdom in the 1830s. At first these missionaries were treated with respect because they were willing to write letters for the king. Many of them also had useful medical and carpentry skills. However, King Mpande soon realized that the missionaries wanted people to obey the laws of Christianity rather than those of the Zulu Kingdom. He forced the missionaries to leave the kingdom in 1842. Their response was to set up mission stations close to the border of the Zulu Kingdom, from which they tried to encourage the king's subjects to cross the border and join them.

The first missionaries who came to convert the Zulu in the 1830s were from the United States.

Within a few years they were joined by missionaries from Britain, Germany, Norway, and Sweden.

The missionaries taught their Zulu converts to read and write and to use improved farming tools. In return, they insisted that Zulu men stop marrying more than one wife and that everyone wear European clothing. The missionaries regarded the clothing worn by the Zulu as inadequate. Young Zulu children often walked around almost naked, while grown men wore skins covering their bodies from the waist to the knee. Married women wore leather skirts and skin or cotton shawls, but these women did not regard it as indecent to leave their breasts exposed. The missionaries mistakenly interpreted Zulu clothing conventions as a sign that the Zulu had no moral values.

EXPANSION OF BRITISH CONTROL

The missionaries were soon followed by large numbers of British settlers, who joined the traders already at Port Natal. In 1843 the port and surrounding land—including areas inhabited by Zulu at the edge of the kingdom—were declared a British colony, known as Natal.

By the early 1850s white settlers had turned much of Natal into large farms. Zulu farmers living in the Natal region were moved by the British onto segregated reserves, many of which were located between Natal and the Zulu Kingdom. Some reserves were controlled by the missionaries.

The Zulu were required to pay taxes to the British. But the reserves were too small for the inhabitants to grow enough food to support themselves and pay the new taxes. This forced many families to work for their white neighbors. Even so, there was a labor shortage on the white-owned farms and sugar plantations of Natal. To solve this problem, the British eventually imported workers from India, which was then also a British colony. Today, descendants of these Indian workers make up a significant percentage of the population of the region.

Missionaries and colonial officials in the Natal region had no authority over the nearby Zulu Kingdom. Hardly anyone who lived in the kingdom ever left it to look for work elsewhere. Instead, they tended their cornfields and animals. Young men still joined the Zulu army, although the

Under the rule of King Mpande the ceremonial uniforms of Zulu soldiers continued to feature beautiful feathers and furs.

military could no longer be used to expand Zulu territory. The kingdom was hemmed in by new white settlements to the north and west in addition to Natal in the south. The Zulu army was also prevented by their better-armed white neighbors from raiding cattle to enrich the kingdom. As a result, King Mpande's possibilities for expanding the kingdom became more and more limited.

THE ZULU CIVIL WAR

In 1856 a civil war broke out in the Zulu Kingdom between Mpande's sons and their supporters. The sons were competing to succeed the aged Mpande, who had not yet made it clear which of his sons was to succeed him as king.

During the war 23,000 Zulu warriors and *civilians* were killed. Six of King Mpande's sons were killed, including one of his favorites, and one son was forced to flee to Natal. Many of the dead were women and children who had drowned in the Thukela River while trying to flee from the fighting. This tragic event upset King Mpande so much that he cried openly when he spoke to visitors about what had happened.

Married women at Dingane's court in beautiful beadwork. During Dingane's reign, beads were expensive, and certain colors were kept for use only by the king and other highly placed people.

With the exception of the tragic civil war of 1856 and the threat posed to the Zulu Kingdom by the growing number of white settlers, everyday life continued more or less as normal throughout the kingdom.

MPANDE'S COURT

At Mpande's court the First Fruits Ceremony was still held every year. The king's royal homestead, Nodwengu (nod-WENG-goo), which was located close to Mgingindhlovu, was still filled with people, including members of the army and the royal family. Also living at Mpande's court were hundreds of young girls who had been given to the king as "daughters" by their families. These young girls were a form of wealth because Mpande received large numbers of *ilobolo* cattle every time he allowed a man to marry one of his "daughters."

We do not know whether the king's adopted daughters were sent to their grooms' homes with the customary presents of headrests, blankets, and cooking pots. We do know, however, that when they left the *isigodlo* they took with them their beautiful and very valuable beaded waistbands, armbands, and necklaces, which they had made from beads given to them by Mpande. The girls were taught the skills of making beadwork by older women in the royal enclosure, including the king's wives and mother.

As in Dingane's era, the king and members of his court continued to wear a great deal of bead-work. However, beads were no longer as rare as they had been in Dingane's time, when certain bead types and colors were associated with the king and others of very high rank. During King Mpande's reign, traders had begun to sell beads and other goods to ordinary people. The only beads that were still associated with royalty were

Detail of a section of Zulu beadwork from the late nineteenth or early twentieth century

large red beads that most people could not afford. However, few people in the kingdom had the time and money to make large quantities of beaded clothing and ornaments. Unlike King Mpande, they never had occasion to wear as many as three different sets of beadwork in a single day.

In addition to their beaded and brass ornaments, Zulu kings all owned beautifully carved thrones. These thrones were never passed on from one king to another. Instead, they were burned after the death of the king, for the same reason that his other personal belongings were burned before his burial.

Many kings also owned chairs made for them by local missionaries. King Dingane had a chair of European manufacture. King Mpande had at least four thrones; two were made by a Norwegian missionary, the other two by a famous Zulu carver. Because anyone visiting the king had to sit on a mat on the floor, he usually looked down on them. These thrones were not used on all occasions, however. Zulu kings also received visitors reclining on mats. On these occasions the king leaned an elbow against a headrest for support.

MPANDE'S DEATH AND HIS LEGACY

Toward the end of his life, King Mpande was so ill that he could no longer walk or sit comfortably. He became obese and had to be taken around in a cart. He died in 1872, the first Zulu king to die of natural causes.

Today, some Zulu people claim that King Mpande was weak. They blame him for allowing settlers and missionaries to sap the power of the kingdom, and for allowing a civil war to develop over the question of who would be the next king. Others remember him with affection as the first Zulu king who loved and acknowledged his children. King Mpande's praises are still always sung at Zulu weddings, in the belief that he has the ability to assist people in their desire to have children.

5 THE DEFEAT OF THE ZULU KINGDOM

After the Zulu civil war of 1856, Mpande's son Cetshwayo emerged as his successor. However, when Cetshwayo came to power in the early 1870s, the Zulu Kingdom had lost its ability to control many of the events that affected it most directly. It was almost completely surrounded by white settlers, who made increasingly unreasonable demands on King Cetshwayo and his people.

Cetshwayo's *coronation* ceremony provides one important example of just how much things had changed in the Zulu Kingdom. In the past, coronations had been organized by the Zulu themselves, but King Cetshwayo's coronation was attended by

King Cetshwayo ruled the Zulu Kingdom from 1872 until the Anglo-Zulu war of 1879.

British officials from Natal who tried to run the whole ceremony. They arrived in the Zulu Kingdom with a large marquee tent, lots of presents for the king, a ridiculous-looking, European-style crown made of tin and feathers that was unlike anything any Zulu king had ever worn before, and a British army band. King Cetshwayo had no choice but to go along with this interference by the British officials.

ONDINI

After his embarrassing coronation, Cetshwayo set about building Ondini, his royal homestead. A huge area of thorn trees and bush was cleared and burned for the site, less than two miles from Mpande's former capital.

Cetshwayo's *isigodlo* included a square, European-style house built of brick. For reasons that are no longer clear, this house was called the black house. King Cetshwayo used it only during the day for meetings with his counselors and visitors. At night, the king still slept in a beehive-shaped Zulu house.

At Ondini, Cetshwayo followed the daily rituals that had been practiced by his predecessors. In the early mornings, the gatekeeper of the *isigodlo* continued to sing the praises of the king. Thereafter, the king often went out hunting with some of his counselors and returned to eat and bathe before receiving visitors. King Cetshwayo is remembered as a king who was always prepared to listen sympathetically to his subjects' problems, even though he was often silent and withdrawn.

One important thing did change at Ondini, however: The king's adopted daughters were taught to shoot with firearms so that they could defend the royal homestead when the men were away. These firearms, which were already quite old, were supplied by a British trader. He lived on the southern border of the Zulu Kingdom surrounded by more than forty Zulu wives and their children. This trader, whose name was John Dunn, became a good friend of King Cetshwayo. He acted as the king's translator and adviser.

THE ANGLO-ZULU WAR

The British wanted to extend Britain's power in southern Africa. There was nothing King Cetshwayo could do to persuade them not to attack his kingdom. He constantly wrote letters assuring the

British government that he had no quarrel with them. They responded by making more and more impossible demands on the king. In 1879, the British declared war.

When war broke out, the Zulu army was so determined to put a permanent stop to Britain's growing threat to their independence that they managed to defeat the British army at Isandlwana, not far from the king's royal homestead. In the end, however, the king's army was not strong enough to withstand the attack of troops with sophisticated handguns and other weapons. When the victorious British troops reached Ondini they burned it to the ground.

CETSHWAYO FLEES

Cetshwayo fled the battle scene and hid in a forest. He was betrayed by the son of a white missionary whom Cetshwayo had once welcomed to Ondini. This young man led the soldiers to the king's hiding place and pointed him out to the British. Cetshwayo felt equally betrayed by his former friend, Dunn, who had turned against the Zulu royal family when the Anglo-Zulu war broke out. He refused to help Cetshwayo in any way.

CETSHWAYO'S LATER YEARS

Once King Cetshwayo had been taken into captivity, he was put on a ship to Cape Town, where he lived for some time before sailing to England in 1882 to petition Queen Victoria to allow him to return to his former home. She was impressed with his charm and intelligence.

In early 1883 King Cetshwayo's wish was granted because he no longer posed any threat to the British. British interference in Zulu affairs had given far greater power and authority to minor Zulu chiefs, who were no longer prepared to obey Cetshwayo. The British had given some of them large areas of land, which they now ruled independently. These rival chiefs were constantly fighting against one another. By dividing the Zulu nation against itself, the British were finally able to destroy the power of Zulu kings. This British strategy, applied in many parts of the British empire, is known as "divide and rule."

King Cetshwayo immediately set about trying to resolve the chaos in the kingdom, but he died suddenly and unexpectedly in early 1884. The British medical officer who examined King Cetshwayo's

King Cetshwayo during his visit to London in 1882, when he asked Queen Victoria and the British government to allow him to return to Zulu country

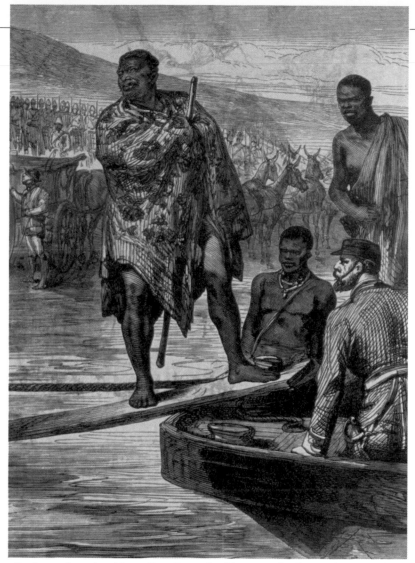

King Cetshwayo boards a ship to Cape Town after his capture by the British. His sudden death soon after being allowed to return to his kingdom aroused suspicion among the Zulu.

body concluded that he had died of a heart attack, but most Zulu-speaking people believe that he was poisoned by his enemies.

6 THE ZULU KINGDOM TODAY

In the 1920s King Cetshwayo's grandson, King Solomon, established an organization aimed at reuniting all Zulu-speakers. He called this the Inkatha movement. The Inkatha movement brought together Zulu-speakers from the former Colony of Natal and the area once known as the Zulu Kingdom. The movement fell apart in the 1930s soon after King Solomon's death.

A new Inkatha movement was established in the 1970s. This movement has played an important role in modern South Africa. It has strong support among the millions of Zulu *migrant laborers* who leave their rural homes in KwaZulu-Natal to work in

South African President Nelson Mandela (left) and Chief Mangosuthu Buthelezi

large cities such as Johannesburg for eleven months of the year. The Inkatha movement revived old Zulu rituals and ceremonies to renew the pride of Zulu-speakers in their warrior heritage.

The president of Inkatha is Chief Mangosuthu Buthelezi. Inkatha encourages its male members to wear furs and feathers, and to carry shields and fighting sticks in imitation of King Shaka's warriors whenever they attend rallies addressed by Buthelezi.

Not all Zulu-speakers belong to Inkatha. Many reject Inkatha because they believe that South Africans should strive to unite across the historical barriers of race, language, and religion. They believe that emphasizing Zulu history and identity can hamper unity.

In 1994, the African National Congress came to power in South Africa, and Nelson Mandela was elected president. Many South Africans believe that Inkatha undermined the search for peace and equality that was started by the new government. It remains to be seen whether Inkatha has a future in a country that is committed to improving the quality of life for all its citizens. Most probably, it will eventually lose its political importance, but will continue to play a significant role in the cultural life of Zulu-speakers.

TIMELINE

A.D. c.1818-28	King Shaka rules the Zulu Kingdom
1824	English traders settle at Port Natal (present-day Durban)
1828	King Shaka is assassinated
1828-1840	King Dingane rules the Zulu Kingdom
1835	Missionaries settle in, and later near, the Zulu Kingdom
1838	King Dingane orders his warriors to kill a party of Boers who had come to his royal homestead to ask for land
1840	King Dingane dies in exile
1840-1873	King Mpande rules the Zulu Kingdom
1843	The British annex Natal
1856	Zulu civil war
1872	King Mpande dies of old age
1872-1879	King Mpande's son, Cetshwayo, rules the Zulu Kingdom
1879	Anglo-Zulu war; King Cetshwayo is captured by the British
1884	After returning to his kingdom, King Cetshwayo dies
1924	First Inkatha movement is founded by King Solomon
1975	Second Inkatha movement is founded by Chief Mangosuthu Buthelezi
1994	The Republic of South Africa becomes a democracy

GLOSSARY

amakhowe large edible mushrooms that grow in the grass-lands of southeast Africa

apartheid the belief, supported by law, that white people are superior to other peoples, who should thus be kept separate from whites and treated as inferiors; the policy of the government of the Republic of South Africa until 1994

Boer "farmer" in Dutch language; white settler of mostly Dutch descent who settled in southern Africa

chiefdom territory ruled by a chief, and the people in it

civilian person who is not part of the military

conscript to draft into the military

coronation ceremony in which a ruler is crowned and officially given authority to rule

creation myth story that explains the creation of the world and humankind

gourd the hard, dried shell of a pumpkin-like plant, used for carrying and storing liquids

homestead family compound made up of several buildings and areas for herd animals

idumbe root vegetable eaten throughout the Zulu kingdom

ilobolo cattle given by a bridegroom to the father of his bride

insulation any material capable of keeping out either the heat or the cold

isigodlo royal enclosure at one end of the king's royal homestead, occupied by the king, his wives, and other members of the royal family

migrant laborer person who regularly travels far from his or her home to work temporarily wherever work is available

nonconformist concerning an attitude or behavior that is unlike that of most people in a society

thatching grass bundles of thick, dry grass sewn onto the wooden frames of Zulu houses

tribute required payment made to the ruler of a nearby country or kingdom

FOR FURTHER READING

Morris, Jean, and Eleanor Preston-White. *Speaking with Beads: Zulu Arts from Southern Africa.* New York: Thames and Hudson, 1994.

Ngwani, Zolani. *Zulu.* New York: Rosen Publishing Group, 1997.

FOR ADVANCED READERS

Omer-Cooper, John D. *History of Southern Africa.* 2nd ed. Portsmouth, NH: Heinemann, 1994.

Webb, Colin, and John Wright, eds. *A Zulu King Speaks: Statements made by Cetshwayo kaMpande on the History and Customs of His People.* Pietermaritzburg: University of Natal Press, 1978.

WEB SITES

Due to the changeable nature of the Internet, sites appear and disappear very quickly. Internet addresses must be entered with capital and lowercase letters exactly as they appear.

Britannica Search—Shaka:
    http://www.eb.com/cgi-bin/g?keywords=Shaka

Eloquent Elegance—Beadwork in the Zulu Cultural Tradition:
    http://minotaur.marques.com.za/clients/zulu/index.htm

Wars of the Region (1836–1902):
    http://atex.co.za/att/heritage/history.html

INDEX

ABOUT THE AUTHOR

Sandra Klopper was born in South Africa. She holds an M.A. from the University of East Anglia and a Ph.D., and is currently a senior lecturer in the Department of History of Art at the University of Cape Town, South Africa. Her dissertation research was on the art of Zulu-speakers living in the area where she had lived as a teenager and where King Dingane and his successors had settled after the death of the first Zulu king, Shaka. Besides lecturing on African art, she teaches courses on the art of the Mexican muralists, the history of advertising, and feminist art from the 1970s.